The
Healthy Protein
KITCHEN

The
Healthy Protein
KITCHEN

*Feel-good food for
happy and healthy eating*

This edition published by Parragon Books Ltd in 2016 and
distributed by

Parragon Inc.
440 Park Avenue South, 13th Floor
New York, NY 10016
www.parragon.com/lovefood

LOVE FOOD is an imprint of Parragon Books Ltd

ISBN 978-1-4748-3804-7

Printed in China

New recipes by Joy Skipper
Introduction by Judith Wills
Cover and new recipe photography by Tony Briscoe
Home economy by Sian Davies

NOTES FOR THE READER

This book uses standard kitchen measuring spoons and cups.
All spoon and cup measurements are level unless otherwise
indicated. Unless otherwise stated, milk is assumed to be
whole, eggs are large, individual vegetables and fruits are
medium, and pepper is freshly ground black pepper, and salt
is table salt. A pinch of salt is calculated as $1/16$ of a teaspoon.
Unless otherwise stated, all root vegetables should be peeled
prior to using.

The times given are an approximate guide only. Preparation
times differ according to the techniques used by different
people, and the cooking times may also vary from those given.

Please note that any ingredients stated as being optional are
not included in the nutritional values provided. The nutritional
values given are approximate and provided as a guideline
only, they do not account for individual cooks, scales, and
portion sizes. The nutritional values provided are per serving
or per item.

CONTENTS

WHAT IS PROTEIN?

Protein is one of the major nutrients our bodies need for health, growth, and normal functioning, and we need to consume it regularly. It is a component of many foods, but it doesn't always take the same form. It consists of combinations of amino acids—often called protein's "building blocks"—that are vital for every metabolic process in our bodies and make up a large proportion of our cells, muscles, and tissue. Protein-containing foods vary in the amount and type of these amino acids that they contain.

Protein is essential for building, maintaining, and repairing cells and for the actual structure of cells. It also helps protect us from viral and bacterial infections and boosts the immune system; acts as a coordinator between various body processes; helps with body movement; and transports atoms and molecules around the body. Surplus protein can also be converted into energy (calories).

Our total protein needs may alter according to our circumstances. Body weight is perhaps the most important factor—adults need around 0.3 gram of protein a day per pound of their weight. Pregnant and breastfeeding women also need more protein than average, while factors such as age and activity levels may alter our optimum intake.

Most adults in the United States, for example, do eat enough protein, according to official figures, but protein deficiency and malnutrition throughout the world is common. High activity levels increase protein needs by up to 50 percent and some research shows that older people may need around 25 percent more protein than younger adults.

While vegetarians don't need more protein than anyone else, they need to get a good daily variety of protein-containing foods so they get all the essential amino acids.

Our recipes include a balanced mixture of natural protein types, including vegetable, meat, fish, and dairy proteins. The vegetable-base recipes aren't necessarily strictly vegetarian or vegan, so make sure you check the ingredients list if you are avoiding meat or animal products.

Your protein intake can be improved by making good choices at any meal of the day. Healthy breakfasts, lunches, snacks, dinners, and desserts that are higher in protein than perhaps your usual choices can help to increase your protein levels.

VEGETABLE-BASE PROTEINS

Vegetable-base protein sources are an excellent choice and provide a range of health and nutritional benefits. When people think of "protein" foods, they often think of animal sources, such as meat and fish. However, it is not difficult to get your daily requirements of protein by choosing more—or even all—from the wide range of vegetable-base foods. These include legumes, such as fresh and dried beans, peas, and lentils, as well as nuts and seeds. Many other types of vegetables are good or useful sources of protein.

Humans need 20 different types of amino acids and the body can manufacture 11 of them. However, the other nine amino acids must come from the diet, so they are called essential (or indispensible). Individual foods that do contain all of the essential amino acids are called "complete proteins."

Few individual vegetable-base protein foods are classified as complete proteins, but all vegetable sources do contain a mixture of some or most of the essential amino acids. If you eat a good variety of vegetable protein sources every day, then you will probably get all of the amino acids you need. Soybeans, quinoa, amaranth, buckwheat, and chia seeds contain all nine essential amino acids and are, therefore, classified as complete proteins.

LEGUMES

Dried beans, peas, and lentils are a major source of protein in a vegetable-base diet, because they are eaten in place of animal protein sources, often with lower-protein carbs, such as rice and potatoes. They are also rich in various vitamins and minerals as well as fiber and plant chemicals.

NUTS AND SEEDS

Although we tend to eat nuts and seeds in smaller quantities, they are a valuable source of protein, and they also contain important unsaturated fats and a variety of vitamins and minerals, fiber, and plant chemicals.

GRAINS AND PSEUDOGRAINS

Rolled oats and whole wheat are popular and traditionally thought of as carb foods, but they are surprisingly high in protein. Other grains, such as spelt, wild rice, quinoa (not actually a grain but a seed), and amaranth contain useful amounts of protein.

VEGETABLES

All plant foods contain at least some protein, and several vegetables supply good amounts, including leafy greens, such as spinach, cabbage, and broccoli, as well as fresh peas and beans.

EGGS AND DAIRY-BASE PROTEINS

Milk, cheese, and yogurt are an important part of a protein-rich diet for many vegetarians, and they are also a great source of calcium, while eggs contain a range of vitamins and minerals.

EGGS

Several research studies on eggs show that a breakfast or meal containing eggs can help reduce hunger throughout the day and limit calorie intake. They are a good source of the B vitamins as well as iron, zinc, and selenium.

Egg whites are cholesterol-free, low-calorie, and 85% protein. An average egg contains only one-third of its fat as saturates, while over one-third are healthy monounsaturates.

If you buy organic eggs from hens allowed unlimited access to organic pastures and woodland, they will have a naturally higher content of omega-3 fats—the healthy unsaturated group also found (in another form) in oily fish—a lower saturates level, and more vitamin E.

MILK AND YOGURT

Milk and yogurt can make a useful contribution to your daily protein intake. Not all milk and yogurt as high in saturated fat as is often thought. For example, regular Greek yogurt contains a higher level of protein than other types of yogurt and its saturated fat content is relatively low.

Milk and yogurt are good sources of calcium, necessary for healthy bones, as well as the B vitamins. Whole milk is also a good source of vitamin A; low-fat versions are not, because the vitamin is found only in the fat.

Sheep and goat milk and yogurt are becoming more popular and more readily available, and some people may find them easier to digest.

CHEESE

Cheese is often thought of as one of the best sources of protein but some varieties have a much higher content than others.

Hard cheeses, such as cheddar, Parmesan, and Gruyère, are some of the best, while creamy and soft cheeses are often low in protein, with the exceptions being soft goat cheese, ricotta, and quark/fromage blanc.

Hard cheeses are a good source of calcium and the B vitamins, while regular (not reduced-fat) cheeses are a good source of vitamin A.

Organic milk, yogurt, and cheese tend to contain a better ratio of healthy unsaturated fats to saturated fats.

Meals and snacks containing cheese help to increase satiety and keep hunger at bay for longer.

MEAT AND FISH PROTEINS

Red and white meats, poultry, and fish have been recommended for decades as the best sources of top-quality complete protein. However, in recent years, there has been much conflicting evidence and advice about how much of them we should eat.

WHAT DOES TOP-QUALITY PROTEIN MEAN?

Top-quality protein refers to a protein source that contains all the essential amino acids in good proportions that are easily absorbed by the digestive system. Animal sources of protein, such as lean meat and fish, are excellent sources of top-quality complete proteins that are well absorbed by most people.

DO WE NEED MEAT AND FISH?

No. Vegetarian and vegan diets can, with care, provide the full range of nutrients. However, vegetables and meat/fish contain different nutrients needed for health (for example, red meat is high in easily absorbed iron and zinc, while legumes contain less; legumes are rich in fiber, while meats contain none; oily fish is a great source of omega-3 fat, while vegetables contain little), so a diet that combines both could be an easy way to be sure you get all the nutrients you need.

However, we shouldn't eat too much red meat (beef, lamb, pork, veal, venison, or goat). Recent advice from health departments across the world is that we should limit our intake to no more than 2 1/2 ounces a day or 17 1/2 ounces a week, because high intake may be linked with bowel cancer.

The best idea is to use it as a small component of a meal instead of "the main event." Because ounce for ounce, meat is higher in protein than most other protein sources, you can eat less and still meet your protein needs.

Chicken (and other birds) don't fall under official advice on limitation. Choose lean chicken and avoid the fatty skin. Turkey breast is an excellent low-fat and high-protein choice.

CAN WE EAT FISH FREELY?

Instead of limiting our intake of fish, advice is that we should try to eat more. Most of us can have as much white fish as we want and at least one 5-ounce portion of omega-3 rich oily fish, such as salmon or mackerel, a week but no more than four. All fish and seafoods are a complete protein source and contain a range of vitamins and minerals.

PROTEIN FOR YOUR HEALTH

Most people realize that protein helps build muscle and keeps us strong, but it also provides a wide range of other benefits for all of your body and your health. Protein is essential for building, maintaining, and repairing cells and for the actual structure of cells. Each of the nine essential amino acids has its own role to play in keeping the body and mind healthy.

THE NINE ESSENTIAL AMINO ACIDS

ISOLEUCINE: Helps produce hemoglobin for healthy blood and aids muscle recovery after exercise. It is found in soybeans, beef, pork, and tuna.

LEUCINE: Promotes growth and healing. It is found in soybeans, beef, pork, tuna.

LYSINE: For a healthy nervous system and hormonal balance. It is found in pork, chicken, cod, sardines.

METHIONINE: Important for fat metabolism as well as muscle and cartilage maintenance; it is also an anti-inflammatory. It is found in tuna, salmon, hard cheese, and nuts.

PHENYLALANINE: Can help prevent depression, maintain memory, and control satiety. It is found in beef, fish, shellfish, cheese, milk, nuts, and soybeans.

THREONINE: Boosts the immune system and helps build collagen for good skin. It is found in turkey, eggs, and soybeans.

TRYPTOPHAN: Helps promote good sleep, as well as helps prevent migraines and depression. It is found in turkey, chicken, shellfish, milk, yogurt, nuts, seeds, and legumes.

VALINE: Essential for muscle development. It is found in turkey, chicken, dairy produce, soybeans, lentils, and black beans.

HISTIDINE: For growth and development, production of blood cells, and circulation. It is found in beef, Parmesan, soybeans, poultry, oily fish, and seeds.

EATING PROTEIN THROUGHOUT THE DAY

It's not difficult to make sure that you get enough protein every day. If you have a varied diet, with a range of different protein sources and plenty of vegetables, salad greens, and fruits in a variety of colors at each meal, you will be getting the complete range of amino acids you need as well as all the vitamins, minerals, fats, fiber, and carbohydrates that are essential for good health. Our recipes offer an exciting selection of meals and snacks for all occasions.

START THE DAY WITH PROTEIN

A high-protein breakfast is the ideal way to start the day. It will keep you feeling full until lunchtime, help your brain feel alert, and is a good chance to pack in the other nutrients that high-protein foods offer.

Many protein foods are quick and easy to cook; eggs really are a perfect breakfast food and, if you add in fruits or vegetables high in vitamin C, they will help the minerals to be better absorbed.

PACK HIGH-PROTEIN PORTABLE SNACKS

If you lead an active life and are always busy or on the run, having one or two high-protein snacks in your bag or case is an easy way to make sure you don't succumb to snacks from the deli that are high in white carbs, sugar, fat, and salt.

Try a bag of unsalted nuts, or take a mixture of nuts and seeds, such as almonds, cashew nuts, pumpkin seeds, and sunflower seeds. Or try a hard-boiled egg or a seed cracker topped with peanut butter.

IDEAS FOR SNACKING AFTER SPORT

If you've been busy working out, running, or on the playing field, it's a good idea to have a high-protein snack with a small amount of carbohydrate added for instant energy replacement.

Make sure your equipment bag contains such a snack: ideas include a healthy smoothie made with milled flaxseed, almond butter, milk, and banana; some cacao nibs mixed with walnuts; an ounce of Gruyère cheese with one small apple; roasted cooked chickpeas sprinkled with paprika.

EASY INGREDIENT SWAPS FOR EVERYDAY MEALS

~ Replace potatoes with mashed or pureed cannellini or lima beans.
~ Replace rice with quinoa.
~ Choose seed crackers instead of bread.
~ Choose buckwheat noodles instead of pasta.
~ Swap croutons on your salad for lightly toasted nuts and seeds.
~ Making a wrap, choose lettuce leaves instead of the bread.

BREAKFASTS

Pea and kale frittatas	20
Oatmeal with hot smoked salmon	22
Crushed edamame and avocado toasts	24
Orange and banana pancakes	26
Roasted almond gingersnap butter	28
Nutty granola sundaes with yogurt and mango	30
Quinoa and cashew nut porridge	32
Fruity puffed quinoa with pumpkin seeds	34
Spinach and nutmeg baked eggs	36
Three-herb and ricotta omelet	38
Berry power smoothie	40
Flaxseed and chia chocolate smoothie	42

PEA AND KALE FRITTATAS

These mini frittatas are really simple to make and packed with protein from all the eggs. Filling them with a delicious combination of peas and kale makes them even more nutritious.

MAKES: 12 FRITTATAS
PREP: 10 MINS, PLUS COOLING   COOK: 25–30 MINS

2 teaspoons butter, for greasing
1 tablespoon olive oil
4 scallions, trimmed and chopped
$^2/_3$ cup frozen peas, thawed
$^3/_4$ cup shredded kale
6 eggs
$^1/_2$ cup milk
crumbled $^2/_3$ cup feta cheese
salt and pepper (optional)

1. Preheat the oven to 350°F. Grease a 12-cup muffin pan and set aside.

2. Heat the olive oil in a skillet and cook the scallions over medium heat for 3–4 minutes, until beginning to soften.

3. Add the peas and kale to the pan and cook for an additional 2–3 minutes.

4. Beat the eggs and milk together in a bowl and season with salt and pepper, if using.

5. Divide the pea-and-kale mixture among the cups in your prepared pan and pour some egg-milk mixture over each one.

6. Sprinkle the feta cheese over the top of each frittata and bake in the preheated oven for 18–20 minutes, until golden and set.

7. Let the frittatas cool for a few minutes, then remove from the pan with a spatula. Eat them warm or cold.

WHY NOT TRY?
Try out different fillings—make your frittatas with bacon and asparagus, or tomato and basil.

PER FRITTATA: 89 CALS | 6.3G FAT | 2.8G SAT FAT | 2.8G CARBS | 1.5G SUGARS | 0.7G FIBER | 5.3G PROTEIN | 120MG SODIUM

OATMEAL WITH HOT SMOKED SALMON

You may think oatmeal is just for a sweet breakfast, but oats taste great combined with savory flavors and provide sustained energy throughout the morning. Adding salmon provides a protein and omega-3 boost.

SERVES: 4
PREP: 10 MINS   COOK: 12–15 MINS

1²/₃ cups rolled oats
1¹/₂ cup milk
2¹/₂ cups water
4 eggs
4 teaspoons creamed horseradish
7 ounces hot smoked salmon, flaked
2 avocados, pitted, peeled, and sliced
freshly milled black pepper (optional)
2 tablespoons pumpkin seeds, toasted, to garnish

1. Put the oats into a saucepan with the milk and water. Bring to a boil and simmer for 4–5 minutes, until thick and creamy.

2. Meanwhile, poach the eggs in a saucepan of simmering water for 4–5 minutes.

3. Stir the creamed horseradish and half the smoked salmon into the oatmeal.

4. Divide the oatmeal among four warm bowls and top each one with slices of avocado, a poached egg, and the remaining salmon.

5. Serve the oatmeal sprinkled with toasted pumpkin seeds and seasoned with pepper, if using.

SOMETHING DIFFERENT
Sautéed mushrooms topped with a fried egg and a sprinkling of chives make a delicious variation.

PER SERVING: 547 CALS | 32.8G FAT | 7.1G SAT FAT | 37.9G CARBS | 6G SUGARS | 9.1G FIBER | 27.7G PROTEIN | 520MG SODIUM

CRUSHED EDAMAME AND AVOCADO TOASTS

Edamame (soybeans) are rich in protein and avocado is full of omega-3 fats. Sprinkled with toasted sunflower seeds and spread over thick slices of sourdough bread, this is a perfect, tasty breakfast.

SERVES: 4
PREP: 10 MINS COOK: 8–10 MINS

¾ cup frozen edamame, thawed
3 tablespoons sunflower seeds
8 slices sourdough bread
2 tablespoons tahini paste
1 tablespoon lime juice
2 avocados, pitted, peeled, and chopped
½ small red onion, thinly sliced
salt and pepper (optional)
2 tablespoons avocado oil, to serve

1. Put the edamame in a microwave-safe container and microwave for 4½ minutes. Let cool for a few minutes before removing the beans.

2. Toast the sunflower seeds in a dry saucepan over medium heat for 2–3 minutes.

3. Toast the sourdough bread on both sides.

4. Put the edamame into a bowl with the tahini, lime juice, and avocado, then coarsely crush with a fork.

5. Spoon the edamame mixture onto the toasts, then sprinkle with the toasted seeds and slices of onion. Season with salt and pepper, if using.

6. Drizzle with avocado oil to serve.

COOK'S TIP
Other protein-rich toast toppers include poached eggs, smoked salmon, hummus, and peppered steak.

PER SERVING: 478 CALS | 28.9G FAT | 3.8G SAT FAT | 43.4G CARBS | 4.4G SUGARS | 9.2G FIBER | 14.7G PROTEIN | 360MG SODIUM

ORANGE AND BANANA PANCAKES

Teff flour is milled from a fine grain grown mainly in Ethiopia, and it is known for its health-boosting and gluten-free properties. It has a subtle nutty flavor and complements pancakes wonderfully.

SERVES: 4
PREP: 5–10 MINS   COOK: 25 MINS

1 cup teff flour
½ teaspoon ground cinnamon
1 teaspoon baking powder
1 egg
¾ cup milk
2 tablespoons unsalted butter, melted
1 banana, peeled and diced
1 tablespoon melted coconut oil

TO SERVE
2 oranges, peeled and divided into sections
1 tablespoon sesame seeds, toasted
maple syrup (optional)

1. Mix the flour, cinnamon, and baking powder together in a large bowl.

2. Whisk the egg and milk together in a separate bowl, then whisk into the flour mixture until smooth; the batter should be the consistency of thick, heavy cream. Add a little more milk, if needed.

3. Stir the melted butter and banana into the pancake batter.

4. Heat the coconut oil in a skillet over medium heat, then spoon in tablespoons of the batter. Cook for 3–4 minutes, until the pancakes are golden underneath, then flip over and cook for an additional 2–3 minutes.

5. Repeat with the remaining batter until you have 12 pancakes.

6. Serve the pancakes topped with the orange sections, a sprinkling of toasted sesame seeds, and a drizzle of maple syrup, if using.

WHY NOT TRY?
These pancakes can be served with other fresh fruits, honey, or a dollop of plain yogurt.

PER SERVING: 315 CALS | 14.1G FAT | 8.2G SAT FAT | 40.2G CARBS | 12.5G SUGARS | 5.1G FIBER | 9G PROTEIN | 160MG SODIUM

ROASTED ALMOND GINGERSNAP BUTTER

Lightly sweetened with molasses and brown sugar, and spiced with both fresh and ground ginger, this healthy nut butter tastes just like gingersnaps. Try it spread on crisp apples as a light snack or have it on toast with sliced pears.

MAKES: 1¹/₃ CUPS
PREP: 10 MINS   COOK: NONE

2¹/₄ cups roasted almonds
2 tablespoons packed light brown sugar
2 tablespoons molasses
1¹/₂ teaspoons grated fresh ginger
¹/₂ teaspoon ground ginger
¹/₄ teaspoon salt
2–3 tablespoons grapeseed oil
1 apple, sliced, to serve (optional)

1. Put the almonds into a food processor and process for 5–10 minutes, until smooth.

2. Add the sugar, molasses, fresh ginger, ground ginger, and salt and process until well combined. With the processor running, add the oil, a little at a time, until you achieve the desired consistency.

3. Serve immediately on a sliced apple, if desired, or refrigerate until ready to use. Almond butter can be stored in the refrigerator for several weeks.

COOK'S TIP
It can take a while for almonds to release their oils so that your almond butter has the consistency you want. Don't give up. Keep processing (giving your food processor a break now and then if it begins to overheat) until you have a smooth, creamy paste, which could take as long as 10 minutes or more.

PER 1¹/₃ CUPS: 2,204 CALS | 182.3G FAT | 14.8G SAT FAT | 110.5G CARBS | 63G SUGARS | 31.2G FIBER | 60.5G PROTEIN | 600MG SODIUM

NUTTY GRANOLA SUNDAES WITH YOGURT AND MANGO

Making your own granola is so easy—and it means you can include the ingredients you like and take out the ones you don't. It is also cheaper than store-bought granola and tastes delicious.

SERVES: 6
PREP: 10– 15 MINS   COOK: 35-40 MINS

1 cup coarsely chopped almonds
²/₃ cup coarsely chopped pecans
¹/₃ cup coarsely chopped cashew nuts
¹/₃ cup sunflower seeds
²/₃ cup pumpkin seeds
2 tablespoons sesame seeds
1¹/₃ cups rolled oats
3 tablespoons coconut oil
3 tablespoons maple syrup
2 teaspoons ground cinnamon
²/₃ cup dried cranberries
¹/₂ cup Greek–style yogurt
1 mango, pitted, peeled, and chopped

1. Preheat the oven to 350°F.

2. Put the nuts into a large bowl with the seeds and oats, then mix well.

3. In a small saucepan, combine the coconut oil with the maple syrup and cinnamon over medium heat. When the coconut oil has melted, remove from the heat and stir into the nut mixture, mixing well.

4. Spread the mixture over a baking sheet and bake in the preheated oven for 30–35 minutes, shaking and stirring from time to time, until golden.

5. Let the granola cool before stirring in the cranberries.

6. Divide the granola among six bowls and serve layered with yogurt and chopped mango.

GO FOR A VARIETY
The choice of nuts and seeds is up to you, but a wide variety is always best to gain the most nutrients available.

PER SERVING: 646 CALS | 44.4G FAT | 10.9G SAT FAT | 52.6G CARBS | 25.9G SUGARS | 9.3G FIBER | 19G PROTEIN | TRACE SODIUM

QUINOA AND CASHEW NUT PORRIDGE

Creamy and delicious porridge doesn't have to be made with oats.
Quinoa provides much more protein and doesn't contain any wheat.
Cashew nuts also add essential minerals, including magnesium and potassium.

SERVES: 4
PREP: 5–10 MINS   COOK: 12–15 MINS

1 cup quinoa
$^{1}/_{4}$ cup coarsely chopped cashew nuts
4$^{1}/_{4}$ cups almond milk
1 vanilla bean, halved and seeds removed
1 apple, grated
1 teaspoon ground cinnamon
1 tablespoon maple syrup
2 tablespoons chia seeds

TO SERVE
$^{3}/_{4}$ cup raspberries
$^{1}/_{3}$ cup blueberries
2 tablespoons pomegranate seeds

1. Put the quinoa into a pan with the nuts, milk, vanilla seeds, apple, cinnamon, and maple syrup. Bring to a boil, then simmer for 10–12 minutes.

2. Stir the chia seeds into the pan and stir well.

3. Spoon the porridge into four bowls and serve topped with the raspberries, blueberries, and pomegranate seeds.

MIX IT UP
Serve this porridge with the fruit and nuts of your choice. Try to use fruits that are in season, such as berries in the summer, and apples and pears through the cooler months.

PER SERVING: 332 CALS | 11G FAT | 1.1G SAT FAT | 49.9G CARBS | 10.7G SUGARS | 9G FIBER | 13.4G PROTEIN | 160MG SODIUM

FRUITY PUFFED QUINOA WITH PUMPKIN SEEDS

Quinoa puffs are a healthy alternative to regular breakfast cereal. Here, apple juice is used to moisten the puffs instead of the more commonly used milk. It makes a particularly refreshing start to the day!

SERVES: 1
PREP: 10 MINS   COOK: NONE

¹/₂ cup puffed quinoa
¹/₂ cup apple juice
1 small banana, thinly sliced
¹/₂ crisp, red apple, sliced into thin wedges
2 teaspoons pumpkin seeds
1 tablespoon honey, for drizzling
2 tablespoons Greek-style yogurt, to serve

1. Put the puffed quinoa into a serving bowl. Stir in the apple juice, making sure the puffs are submerged. Let stand for a few minutes.

2. Arrange the banana slices and apple wedges on top of the quinoa.

3. Sprinkle with the pumpkin seeds and drizzle with a little honey. Serve immediately with yogurt.

WHY NOT TRY?
For a delicious variation, try using freshly squeezed orange juice instead of the apple juice. You could also replace the apples with pears.

PER SERVING: 393 CALS | 5.1G FAT | 1.7G SAT FAT | 84.6G CARBS | 50.5G SUGARS | 5.7G FIBER | 7G PROTEIN | TRACE SODIUM

SPINACH AND NUTMEG BAKED EGGS

Nutrient-rich fresh spinach adds delicious flavor and color to this popular egg dish, lightly seasoned with ground nutmeg. Serve with standard or gluten-free bread for a wholesome breakfast or brunch.

SERVES: 4

PREP: 20 MINS   COOK: 20–30 MINS

1 tablespoon olive oil, for brushing
1 tablespoon olive oil, for frying
4 shallots, finely chopped
3 garlic cloves, sliced
3½ cups baby spinach
8 eggs
½ teaspoon ground nutmeg
salt and pepper (optional)

1. Preheat the oven to 350°F. Lightly brush the insides of four 1-cup ramekins (individual ceramic dishes) with olive oil.

2. Heat the olive oil in a skillet. Once hot, add the shallots and garlic and sauté over medium heat for 3–4 minutes, or until soft. Add the baby spinach and stir for 2–3 minutes, or until just wilted. Season with salt and pepper, if using.

3. Spoon the spinach mixture into the bottom of the prepared ramekins and crack two eggs into each. Sprinkle with the nutmeg and place the ramekins in a roasting pan. Fill the roasting pan with boiling water until the water reaches halfway up the ramekins—this creates a steamy environment for the eggs so there is no chance of them drying out.

4. Carefully transfer the roasting pan to the preheated oven for 15–20 minutes. Let the ramekins cool slightly, then serve immediately.

SUPER SPINACH

Researchers have found many flavonoid compounds in spinach act as antioxidants and fight against stomach, skin, breast, prostate, and other cancers.

PER SERVING: 235 CALS | 16.5G FAT | 4.2G SAT FAT | 7.5G CARBS | 1.6G SUGARS | 1.1G FIBER | 14.2G PROTEIN | 160MG SODIUM

THREE-HERB AND RICOTTA OMELET

Vibrant green mixed garden herbs add plenty of lovely natural flavor and color to this appetizing omelet. Served with fresh bread to accompany, it fits the bill for a satisfying breakfast for two.

SERVES: 2
PREP: 15 MINS   COOK: 8 MINS

4 extra-large eggs
2 tablespoons finely snipped fresh chives
2 tablespoons finely chopped fresh basil
2 tablespoons finely chopped fresh parsley
⅓ cup crumbled ricotta cheese
2 tablespoons olive oil
salt and pepper (optional)

1. Crack the eggs into a small mixing bowl and lightly beat with a fork. Stir the herbs and ricotta into the bowl and season with salt and pepper, if using.

2. Heat the olive oil in a nonstick skillet over high heat until hot. Pour in the egg mixture and, using a spatula, draw the outside edges (which will cook more quickly) toward the gooey center. Let any liquid mixture move into the gaps. Continue with this action for 4–5 minutes. The omelet will continue to cook once the pan is removed from the heat.

3. Cut the omelet in half and divide between two plates. Serve immediately.

EXCELLENT EGGS
Eggs contain high-quality protein, the macronutrient that best satisfies hunger. They also contain essential vitamins, including vitamin A, needed for healthy skin and good vision.

PER SERVING: 390 CALS | 32G FAT | 10G SAT FAT | 2.8G CARBS | 0.7G SUGARS | 0.2G FIBER | 21.7G PROTEIN | 240MG SODIUM

BERRY POWER SMOOTHIE

Breakfast is arguably the most important meal of the day, and this shake includes loads of vital nutrients. It's quick to make, tasty, and filling, but it won't leave you feeling heavy.

SERVES: 1

PREP: 15 MINS   COOK: NONE

2 tablespoons pumpkin seeds
2 tablespoons flaxseed
3 tablespoons slivered almonds
1 cup raspberries
¾ cup blueberries
1 cup vanilla soy yogurt
½ cup chilled water

1. Put the pumpkin seeds, flaxseed, and almonds into a blender and blend until finely ground.

2. Add the raspberries, blueberries, yogurt, and chilled water and blend until smooth.

3. Pour into a glass and serve.

POWERFUL PUMPKIN SEEDS
These little seeds are really nutritious and, even in small servings, they provide a significant amount of minerals, especially zinc and iron.

PER SERVING: 641 CALS | 33.8G FAT | 3.7G SAT FAT | 72.7G CARBS | 41.8G SUGARS | 19.9G FIBER | 22.1G PROTEIN | 40MG SODIUM

FLAXSEED AND CHIA CHOCOLATE SMOOTHIE

A chocolate smoothie sounds indulgent, but this recipe includes nutritious ingredients, such as flaxseed for added fiber, chia seeds for omega-3 fats, and a raw egg for that extra boost of protein.

SERVES: 2
PREP: 5 MINS   COOK: NONE

1¼ cups milk
1 banana, peeled and chopped
2 teaspoons ground flaxseed
1 teaspoon ground chia seeds
1 tablespoon cacao powder
1 egg

1. Put all the ingredients into a blender and blend until smooth.

2. Pour the smoothie into two glasses and serve.

DID YOU KNOW?
While eggs are a rich source of protein, infants, the elderly, pregnant women, and anyone with a weakened immune system should avoid eating raw eggs.

PER SERVING: 210 CALS | 9.6G FAT | 4G SAT FAT | 24G CARBS | 14.9G SUGARS | 4G FIBER | 9.8G PROTEIN | 80MG SODIUM

LUNCHES AND SNACKS

SALMON AND SOYBEAN SALAD

Salmon is a real superfood—not only is it delicious but it is rich in protein and omega-3 fats, which are important for physical and mental health.

SERVES: 4
PREP: 15 MINS   COOK: 6–8 MINS

14 ounces salmon fillets
1⅓ cups frozen soybeans, thawed
1⅓ cups frozen peas, thawed
½ cup roasted red pepper strips
1½ cups fresh arugula
⅓ cup chopped fresh dill
pepper (optional)

DRESSING
3 tablespoons olive oil
1½ tablespoons lemon juice
1 teaspoon whole-grain mustard
1 teaspoon honey

1. For the dressing, whisk together the olive oil, lemon juice, mustard, and honey in a small bowl. Set aside.

2. Broil the salmon under medium heat for 3–4 minutes on each side, until the fish is opaque and flaky when separated with a fork. Break into large flakes.

3. Meanwhile, bring a large saucepan of water to a boil and add the soybeans and peas to the water. Cook for 3–4 minutes, until just tender. Drain and run under cold water to refresh.

4. Put the salmon flakes, beans, peas, pepper strips, arugula, and dill into a large bowl. Pour the dressing over the top and season with pepper, if using. Toss well to combine. Divide among four bowls and serve.

ALSO TRY ...
Other beans, such as canned cannellini beans or lima beans, work perfectly in this recipe.

PER SERVING: 446 CALS | 30.3G FAT | 5.2G SAT FAT | 13G CARBS | 5.8G SUGARS | 5.1G FIBER | 29.9G PROTEIN | 120MG SODIUM

HARISSA CHICKEN SALAD

Capture the flavors and colors of Morocco with this spicy brown rice salad flecked with jewel-like diced dried apricots and glistening raisins, tossed with health-boosting green kale.

SERVES: 4
PREP: 10–15 MINS   COOK: 30–35 MINS

1⅓ cups quick-cooking brown rice
2 teaspoons tomato paste
1 pound 2 ounces skinless, boneless chicken breasts
½ cup diced dried apricots
⅓ cup raisins
½ preserved lemon, drained and finely chopped
1 small red onion, finely chopped
1¼ cups shredded kale
3 tablespoons pine nuts, toasted

DRESSING
2 teaspoons harissa
¼ cup olive oil
juice of 1 lemon
salt and pepper (optional)

1. Put the rice into a saucepan of boiling water. Bring back to a boil, then simmer for 25–30 minutes, or until tender. Drain, then transfer to a salad bowl.

2. Meanwhile, to make the dressing, put the harissa, oil, and lemon juice in a screw-top jar, season with salt and pepper, if using, screw on the lid, and shake well.

3. Spoon 2 tablespoons of the dressing into a bowl and mix in the tomato paste. Preheat the broiler to high and line the broiler pan with aluminum foil. Put the chicken onto the foil in a single layer. Brush some of the tomato dressing over the chicken, then broil for 15–18 minutes, or until golden and cooked through, turning the meat and brushing it with the remaining tomato dressing halfway through cooking. Cut through the middle of a breast to check that the meat is no longer pink and any juices run clear and are piping hot. Cover and let cool.

4. Drizzle the remaining dressing over the rice in the salad bowl. Add the dried apricots, raisins, preserved lemon, and onion, then toss gently together and let cool.

5. Add the kale and pine nuts to the salad and stir well. Thinly slice the chicken, arrange it over the salad, and serve.

HEALTH-GIVING RICE
Rice is an important source of protein and energy. Quick-cooking brown rice has a little of the bran removed and is parboiled before milling, speeding up cooking but retaining far more of the vital nutrients and fiber than white rice. Homeopaths believe that rice can help treat digestive disorders, from indigestion to diverticulitis.

PER SERVING: 668 CALS | 24G FAT | 3.1G SAT FAT | 78.8G CARBS | 22.1G SUGARS | 6.4G FIBER | 36.3G PROTEIN | 360MG SODIUM

POKE BOWL

A poke bowl is a staple Hawaiian dish that normally contains raw fish and plenty of vibrant ingredients, both hot and cold. This recipe includes tuna for protein and wakame for magnesium, iodine, and calcium.

SERVES: 4
PREP: 15 MINS, PLUS SOAKING   COOK: 25 MINS

1 cup brown rice
³/₄ cup wakame, soaked in lukewarm water for
10–15 minutes and coarsely chopped
2 tablespoons soy sauce
2 tablespoons rice wine vinegar
8 ounces good-quality raw tuna, sliced
1 avocado, pitted, peeled, and sliced
8 cherry tomatoes, halved
4 scallions, thinly sliced
¹/₂ teaspoon crushed red pepper flakes
2 tablespoons olive oil
1 tablespoon black sesame seeds

1. Cook the rice according to the package directions.

2. Put the cooked rice into a bowl and stir in half the soaked wakame, half the soy sauce, and the rice wine vinegar. Divide among four bowls and top with the tuna, avocado, tomatoes, and scallions.

3. Mix the remaining soy sauce and wakame with the crushed red pepper flakes, olive oil, and sesame seeds in a small bowl. Sprinkle the topping over the poke bowls to serve.

A FLASH IN THE PAN
If you don't want to eat your fish raw, flash-fry it quickly in a pan before adding to your dish.

PER SERVING: 399 CALS | 15.4G FAT | 2.2G SAT FAT | 45.5G CARBS | 2.4G SUGARS | 5.3G FIBER | 20.4G PROTEIN | 520MG SODIUM

CHICKEN NOODLE PROTEIN SOUP

This classic chicken soup is an easy, nutritious lunch and can be made in advance. It's full of health benefits—red chiles lower cholesterol and soba noodles are made from gluten-free buckwheat flour.

SERVES: 4

PREP: 20 MINS   COOK: 20 MINS

4¹/₄ cups chicken broth
1 tablespoon soy sauce
1 garlic clove, crushed
1 red chile, seeded and finely chopped
1¹/₄-inch piece fresh ginger, peeled and grated
1 pound 2 ounces skinless, boneless chicken breasts
4 eggs
14 ounces soba noodles
²/₃ cup corn kernels
4 small bok choys, cut lengthwise into quarters
1 tablespoon sesame oil, for drizzling

1. Put the broth, soy sauce, garlic, chile, and ginger into a saucepan and bring to a boil. Add the chicken and simmer for 10–12 minutes, until the chicken is tender and the juices run clear when the tip of a sharp knife is inserted into the thickest part of the meat. Remove the chicken with a slotted spoon.

2. Meanwhile, boil the eggs for 4–5 minutes in a saucepan of boiling water. Refresh under cold water. Drain and peel the eggs.

3. Return the broth to the heat, bring to a simmer, and add the noodles. Cook for 2 minutes, or according to the package directions. Add the corn and bok choy, and simmer for an additional 2 minutes.

4. Shred or thickly slice the chicken and return to the pan with the broth and noodles to heat through for 1 minute.

5. Serve the soup in four warm bowls with halved soft-boiled eggs on top and drizzled with the sesame oil.

WHY NOT TRY?
You can make this soup with a mixture of fish broth, white fish, and shrimp if you don't want chicken.

PER SERVING: 677 CALS | 14.3G FAT | 3.3G SAT FAT | 80.7G CARBS | 12.2G SUGARS | 5G FIBER | 52.7G PROTEIN | 1,200MG SODIUM

LENTIL AND CHICKPEA SOUP

Mixing vegetable proteins, such as rice and lentils, is the best way to get all of the essential amino acids. This soup has a variety of vegetables, plus loads of tantalizing spices for nutrition and flavor.

SERVES: 4
PREP: 10 MINS   COOK: 25 MINS

¾ cup brown rice
2 teaspoons cumin seeds
¼ teaspoon crushed red pepper flakes
1½ tablespoons melted coconut oil, for frying
1 red onion, peeled and chopped
¾ cup red split lentils
3½ cups vegetable broth
1⅔ cups canned diced tomatoes
1½ cups drained and rinsed, canned chickpeas
4 scallions, trimmed and sliced
1 cup drained and rinsed, canned green lentils or cooked green lentils
salt and pepper (optional)
¼ cup Greek-style yogurt, to serve
⅓ cup fresh cilantro leaves, to serve

1. Cook the rice according to the package directions.

2. Meanwhile, cook the cumin seeds and crushed red pepper flakes in a dry saucepan over medium heat for 1 minute before adding 1 tablespoon of the coconut oil.

3. Add the red onion to the saucepan and cook for 3–4 minutes. Stir in the red lentils, broth, tomatoes, and half the chickpeas, then bring to a boil. Simmer for 15 minutes, until the lentils have softened.

4. Meanwhile, heat the remaining oil in a separate saucepan and sauté the scallions over medium heat for 3–4 minutes before stirring in the green lentils. Cook for 1–2 minutes to heat through.

5. Using a handheld blender, blend the soup in the saucepan until smooth. Season with salt and pepper, if using.

6. Pour the soup into four warm bowls and add a spoonful of rice, the remaining chickpeas, the scallions, and green lentils to each one. Serve topped with a dollop of yogurt and a sprinkling of cilantro.

LOVELY LENTILS
Lentils are a rich source of fiber, which helps protect against cancer and cardiovascular disease.

PER SERVING: 457 CALS | 11G FAT | 6.3G SAT FAT | 71.4G CARBS | 7.4G SUGARS | 10.3G FIBER | 19.7G PROTEIN | 800MG SODIUM

ZUCCHINI AND BEAN TACOS

Tacos and homemade guacamole can be a delicious snack or light lunch. This recipe includes a salad made with cannellini beans for protein, plus crunchy celery, carrot, and zucchini for extra fiber.

SERVES: 4
PREP: 12 MINS, PLUS COOLING   COOK: 30 MINS

TACO SHELLS
2 zucchini, grated
1⅓ cups freshly grated Parmesan cheese
2 cups fresh bread crumbs
2 eggs, beaten
salt and pepper (optional)

GUACAMOLE
1 red chile, seeded and finely diced
juice of ½ lime
2 ripe avocados, pitted and peeled

TACO FILLING
2 celery stalks, thinly sliced
1 zucchini, diced
1 carrot, peeled and grated
1 small red onion, peeled and diced
3 cups drained and rinsed, canned cannellini beans
8 cherry tomatoes, quartered
2 tablespoons chopped fresh cilantro
2 tablespoons extra virgin olive oil

TO SERVE
1 cup fresh watercress
¼ cup plain yogurt
2 tablespoons pumpkin seeds, toasted

1. Preheat the oven to 400°F. Line two baking sheets with nonstick parchment paper and set aside.

2. To make the taco shells, wrap the grated zucchini in paper towels and squeeze as much moisture from them as possible. Mix the zucchini, cheese, bread crumbs, and eggs together in a bowl. Season with salt and pepper, if using.

3. Spread the mixture into eight circles on the prepared baking sheets. Bake in the preheated oven for 20 minutes.

4. Turn the taco shells over and bake for an additional 10 minutes, then remove from the baking sheets and lay over a rolling pin to help them curl. Let cool.

5. Meanwhile, make the guacamole. Put the chile, lime juice, and avocados into a small bowl and mash together until smooth. Set aside.

6. To make the taco filling, mix together the celery, zucchini, carrot, onion, beans, tomatoes, cilantro, and olive oil in a bowl.

7. Divide the watercress among the cooled taco shells, then spoon the bean mixture into each one.

8. Top each taco with a dollop of guacamole and yogurt, and sprinkle with toasted pumpkin seeds to serve.

HEALTHY ZUCCHINI
Zucchini provide immune system–boosting vitamin C and significant levels of potassium, which help control blood pressure.

PER SERVING: 621 CALS | 33G FAT | 9.3G SAT FAT | 50.3G CARBS | 10.6G SUGARS | 17.4G FIBER | 31.2G PROTEIN | 640MG SODIUM

SPICY PARSNIP YOGURT WITH FLATBREADS

Thick yogurt is transformed into a wonderful dip by stirring in a parsnip puree and topping with spices and herbs. The flatbreads are made from ground chickpeas for increased protein and fiber.

SERVES: 4
PREP: 15 MINS, PLUS STANDING   COOK: 40–50 MINS

1 large parsnip, peeled and chopped
1³/₄ cups Greek-style yogurt
1 tablespoon harrisa paste
2 tablespoons rinsed canned chickpeas
1 tablespoon snipped fresh chives
2 extra-large egg whites

FLATBREADS

2³/₄ cups chickpea (besan) flour
¹/₃ cup plus 1 tablespoon buckwheat flour
1 teaspoon baking powder
1 teaspoon cumin seeds
1³/₄ cups water
1 tablespoon olive oil, for frying
salt and pepper (optional)

1. To make the flatbreads, put the flours, baking powder, and cumin in a large bowl. Season with salt and pepper, if using. Whisk in the water until smooth. Set aside for 90 minutes so the mixture can soak up the water.

2. Meanwhile, cook the parsnip in a saucepan of boiling water for 12–15 minutes, until soft. Drain and blend to a puree in a small blender.

3. Mix the yogurt and harissa paste in a bowl, leaving swirls of both (do not combine completely). Sprinkle with the chickpeas and chives.

4. When the flatbread batter is ready, whisk the egg whites in a small bowl until stiff. Fold them into the flatbread batter.

5. Heat the olive oil in a large skillet and pour in one-quarter of the batter. Cook for 3–4 minutes over medium heat, until the top starts to bubble and the bottom is golden. Flip over and cook for an additional 3–4 minutes, until golden on both sides. Remove from the pan and repeat with the remaining batter.

6. Serve the flatbreads with the spicy parsnip yogurt.

MAKE IT SWEET
The flatbread can also be turned into a sweet bread—omit the pepper and stir in 1 teaspoon of sugar instead.

PER SERVING: 472 CALS | 14.1G FAT | 4.6G SAT FAT | 58.9G CARBS | 13.7G SUGARS | 10.9G FIBER | 27.6G PROTEIN | 240MG SODIUM

BLACK RICE AND POMEGRANATE BOWL

This colorful bowl is full of flavor and bursting with protein-rich lima beans, black rice, and cottage cheese. Kale and butternut squash also provide antioxidants to keep you happy and healthy.

SERVES: 4

PREP: 15 MINS COOK: 25 MINS

1 small butternut squash, seeded and diced
1 red onion, peeled and sliced
1 tablespoon olive oil
2/3 cup black rice
1 cup shredded kale
2 tablespoons pine nuts
1 2/3 cups drained and rinsed, canned lima beans
1/4 cup cottage cheese, to serve
seeds from 1 pomegranate, to serve

DRESSING

1/4 cup tahini paste
juice of 1 lemon
1 garlic clove, crushed
2 tablespoons extra virgin olive oil

1. Preheat the oven to 400°F.

2. Put the butternut squash and onion onto a roasting pan and drizzle with the olive oil. Roast in the preheated oven for 15 minutes.

3. Cook the rice according to the package directions.

4. Meanwhile, add the kale and pine nuts to the squash and roast for an additional 10 minutes. Remove from the oven and toss in the lima beans.

5. To make the dressing, whisk the tahini, lemon juice, garlic, and olive oil together in a small bowl. Set aside.

6. Drain the rice and divide among four warm bowls. Spoon the roasted vegetables and nuts over the rice, and add a dollop of cottage cheese and sprinkling of pomegranate seeds.

7. Drizzle the dressing into each bowl to serve.

VITAMIN C BOOST

For even more color and extra vitamin C, add red and yellow bell peppers to the roasting pan with the squash.

PER SERVING: 492 CALS | 23.7G FAT | 3.3G SAT FAT | 58.7G CARBS | 10.7G SUGARS | 10.5G FIBER | 14.8G PROTEIN | 80MG SODIUM

CHICKPEA TOFU STICKS WITH SPICY DIP

Cottage cheese is a fresh curd that's drained but not pressed, so some of the whey remains. As the base of a spicy dip, it tastes amazing dunked over strips of homemade tofu.

SERVES: 4
PREP: 15 MINS, PLUS STANDING AND CHILLING
COOK: 5–6 MINS

1 cup chickpea (besan) flour
1 teaspoon miso paste
½ teaspoon ground turmeric
2 cups water

SPICY DIP
1⅓ cups cottage cheese
1 tablespoon mayonnaise
2 teaspoons creamed horseradish
½ teaspoon Dijon mustard
1 scallion, trimmed and finely chopped
12 olives, pitted and finely chopped

1. To make the chickpea tofu, put the chickpea (besan) flour into a bowl with the miso paste and turmeric. Whisk in 1 cup of the water.

2. Bring the remaining water to a boil in a saucepan. When the water is boiling, pour the chickpea (besan) flour mix into the pan and start whisking.

3. Simmer while stirring constantly, until the mixture thickens. Pour it into a 6-inch square pan or dish. Let stand at room temperature for 20 minutes, then chill in the refrigerator for at least 30 minutes.

4. Meanwhile, make the dip by combining the ingredients in a small bowl.

5. Cut the tofu into strips and serve with the spicy dip.

SPEEDY DIP
For a really quick dip, stir pesto through cottage cheese and top with Parmesan cheese shavings.

PER SERVING: 208 CALS | 8.9G FAT | 1.9G SAT FAT | 18.7G CARBS | 5.9G SUGARS | 3.2G FIBER | 13.3G PROTEIN | 440MG SODIUM

RAW NUTTY PROTEIN BALLS

These addictive little balls are the perfect postexercise snack.
The assorted nuts and seeds provide loads of protein and minerals,
while the glucose from the dried fruit replenishes energy levels.

MAKES: 16 BALLS
PREP: 6 MINS, PLUS CHILLING   COOK: NONE

1 cup ground almonds (almond meal)
¾ cup cashew nuts
¼ cup dried apricots
2 pitted dried dates
seeds from ½ vanilla pod
4 teaspoons chia seeds
1½ tablespoons coconut oil, melted

1. Put the ground almonds, cashew nuts, apricots, dates, vanilla seeds, and chia seeds in a food processor and process until completely broken down.

2. With the machine running, pour in the coconut oil and process until the mixture starts to come together.

3. Roll the mixture into 16 balls, using your hands. Place them on a plate and chill in the refrigerator for at least 30 minutes.

UP THE ANTI
For a treat and extra antioxidants, cover the balls in melted dark chocolate before putting them into the refrigerator.

PER BALL: 103 CALS | 7.7G FAT | 1.8G SAT FAT | 7.5G CARBS | 4.1G SUGARS | 1.6G FIBER | 2.8G PROTEIN | TRACE SODIUM

PINK
ENERGY BARS

The fun hidden ingredient in these bars is the beet. Beets are an excellent source of folate and is full of magnesium, fiber, vitamin C, iron, vitamin B6, manganese, potassium, and copper—a bundle of goodness!

MAKES: 10 BARS
PREP: 6 MINS, PLUS CHILLING   COOK: NONE

½ cup rolled oats
½ cup ground almonds (almond meal)
2 tablespoons smooth peanut butter
1 small cooked beet
1 tablespoon maple syrup

1. Put the oats into a food processor and process until broken down.

2. Add the remaining ingredients to the processor and process again until the mixture comes together.

3. Press the dough into a 5-inch square pan and smooth the top. Chill in the refrigerator for 1 hour, then cut into bars.

SWEET ENOUGH?
If you're in the mood for something a little less sweet, omit the maple syrup and add salt and pepper instead.

PER BAR: 76 CALS | 4.6G FAT | 0.6G SAT FAT | 7.1G CARBS | 2.4G SUGARS | 1.4G FIBER | 2.6G PROTEIN | TRACE SODIUM

NUT AND BERRY BARS

You can eat these bars for breakfast, a midafternoon snack, or after-dinner dessert. The molasses oozes with iron, calcium, and magnesium, and the goji berries contain protein and fiber.

MAKES: 12 BARS
PREP: 12 MINS   COOK: 24–26 MINS

2 teaspoons butter, for greasing
1/2 cup coconut oil
1/4 cup molasses
1 1/2 tablespoons packed light brown sugar
3 tablespoons agave syrup
2 2/3 cups rolled oats
2 1/2 tablespoons instant dry milk
1/3 cup coarsely chopped pecans
6 Brazil nuts, coarsely chopped
3 tablespoons goji berries

1. Preheat the oven to 350°F. Grease a 7-inch square pan and set aside.

2. In a large saucepan, melt the coconut oil over medium heat with the molasses, sugar, and agave syrup. Stir until the sugar has dissolved.

3. Pour the remaining ingredients into the pan and mix together well.

4. Pour the batter into the prepared pan and level the top.

5. Bake for 18–20 minutes in the preheated oven. Remove from the oven and let cool completely before cutting into squares.

WHY NOT TRY?
Goji berries are available from most supermarkets and health food stores, but you can substitute them with dried cranberries, which also have a great flavor.

PER BAR: 242 CALS | 14.9G FAT | 8.2G SAT FAT | 23.5G CARBS | 9.1G SUGARS | 2.8G FIBER | 4G PROTEIN | TRACE SODIUM

ORANGE
PROTEIN BARS

Chickpeas are rich in protein, full of fiber, and provide essential minerals, such as potassium, which is important for preventing muscle cramps. Mixed with citrusy orange zest, they make delicious snack bars.

MAKES: 10 BARS
PREP: 12 MINS, PLUS CHILLING   COOK: NONE

2 teaspoons butter, for greasing
1²/₃ cup drained and rinsed, canned chickpeas,
7 dates, pitted
1 tablespoon ground flaxseed
2 tablespoons almond butter
½ teaspoon ground cinnamon
grated zest of 1 orange
2 tablespoons chopped candied peel

1. Grease and line the bottom of a 6-inch square pan with wax paper. Set aside.

2. Put the chickpeas, dates, flaxseed, almond butter, cinnamon, and orange zest into a food processor and process until the mixture breaks down and starts to come together.

3. Stir the candied peel into the processor.

4. Spoon the dough into the prepared pan and smooth the top. Chill in the refrigerator for 1 hour, then remove from the pan and cut into bars.

LOVELY FLAXSEED
Flaxseed are naturally gluten-free, a rich source of omega-3 essential fatty acids, and a good source of fiber.

PER BAR: 83 CALS | 3.4G FAT | 0.8G SAT FAT | 10.8G CARBS | 5.9G SUGARS | 2.7G FIBER | 2.4G PROTEIN | 40MG SODIUM

MAIN DISHES

WHOLE-WHEAT LINGUINE WITH MARINATED TOFU

Tofu is a soy-base protein that can be used in stir-fries and other vegetarian dishes. It doesn't have a strong flavor, so making a marinade with garlic, honey, and chile makes it even tastier.

SERVES: 4
PREP: 15 MINS, PLUS MARINATING   COOK: 15 MINS

¾ cup tofu cubes
12 ounces whole-wheat linguine
1 tablespoon olive oil, for frying
2 cups sliced cremini mushrooms
2 fresh thyme sprigs, leaves only
juice of ½ lemon
salt and pepper (optional)
2 tablespoons chopped fresh parsley, to garnish
2 tablespoons freshly grated Parmesan cheese, to garnish

MARINADE
1 tablespoon olive oil
juice and zest of ½ lime
1 garlic clove, crushed
¼ teaspoon crushed red pepper flakes
2 tablespoons soy sauce
2 tablespoons honey

1. To make the marinade, mix all the marinade ingredients together in a large bowl. Add the cubes of tofu, making sure each piece is coated in the mixture. Let marinate for at least 30 minutes.

2. Cook the linguine according to the package directions.

3. Meanwhile, heat the olive oil in a skillet and cook the mushrooms for 5–6 minutes over medium heat. Toss in the thyme leaves and lemon juice just before removing from the heat.

4. Heat a ridged grill pan until hot and cook the tofu over medium heat for 5–6 minutes, until golden.

5. Drain the pasta and transfer it to a large bowl with the mushroom mixture and tofu. Season with salt and pepper, if using. Toss together.

6. Serve the pasta garnished with chopped parsley and grated cheese.

MARVELOUS MUSHROOMS
Mushrooms are an ideal source of healthy protein for vegetarians and vegans.

PER SERVING: 463 CALS | 12.2G FAT | 2G SAT FAT | 77.6G CARBS | 12.3G SUGARS | 8.7G FIBER | 18.1G PROTEIN | 480MG SODIUM

SALMON QUINOA BURGERS

Made with salmon, quinoa, and egg, these burgers are full of protein. Topped with spicy mayonnaise and a spritz of lime juice, you'll find it difficult to find a tastier burger.

SERVES: 4
PREP: 15 MINS, PLUS CHILLING   COOK: 20–25 MINS

3/4 cup quinoa
9 3/4 ounces cooked salmon, broken into flakes
1 egg, beaten
4 scallions, trimmed and sliced
1 tablespoon chopped fresh cilantro
4 whole-wheat burger buns
1 tablespoon olive oil, for frying
12 fresh watercress sprigs
1/4 cucumber, sliced
salt and pepper (optional)
4 lime wedges, to serve

SPICY MAYONNAISE
2 tablespoons capers, chopped
1/4 cup mayonnaise
juice of 1/2 lime

1. Bring a large saucepan of water to a boil. Add the quinoa and boil for 8–10 minutes. Drain well.

2. Put the quinoa into a bowl with the salmon, egg, scallions, and cilantro. Season with salt and pepper, if using, and mix well.

3. With your hands, shape the mixture into four patties. Place them on a plate and chill in the refrigerator for 20 minutes.

4. Meanwhile, make the spicy mayonnaise. Mix the capers, mayonnaise, and lime juice together in a small bowl. Set aside.

5. Halve and toast the burger buns.

6. Heat the olive oil in a skillet and cook the patties over medium heat for 4–5 minutes on each side, until golden.

7. Spread the spicy mayonnaise over the bottom burger halves with a few sprigs of watercress and some slices of cucumber. Top with the burgers and sandwich with the second bun halves.

8. Serve the burgers with lime wedges.

SUPER SALMON
Salmon is an excellent source of omega-3 fats, cancer-fighting selenium, and vitamin B_{12}, which help protect against heart disease and chronic diseases, such as Alzheimer's disease, depression, and diabetes.

PER SERVING: 542 CALS | 27.3G FAT | 4.4G SAT FAT | 48.7G CARBS | 4.1G SUGARS | 4G FIBER | 26.1G PROTEIN | 480MG SODIUM

BUTTERNUT SQUASH AND LENTIL BOWL

Most plant-base foods do not include all the essential amino acids that make up protein in one ingredient, but lentils and rice will make a complete protein meal. To further increase the protein content, use all wild rice.

SERVES: 4
PREP: 10 MINS   COOK: 50 MINS

2 butternut squash
2 tablespoons olive oil
3/4 cup brown basmati and wild rice
1 teaspoon coconut oil, melted
4 scallions, trimmed and sliced
1 1/4-inch piece fresh ginger, grated
1 lemongrass stalk, trimmed and finely sliced
1 tablespoon Thai green curry paste
1 3/4 cups canned coconut milk
2 cups canned or cooked green lentils
1 1/2 cups chopped Tuscan kale or black-leaf kale
1 tablespoon golden sesame seeds
1 tablespoon black sesame seeds
1/4 cup fresh cilantro leaves, to garnish

1. Preheat the oven to 400°F.

2. Halve the squash, scoop out the seeds, and score the flesh with a sharp knife.

3. Place the four squash halves on a baking pan and drizzle with olive oil. Roast in the preheated oven for 40 minutes. Meanwhile, cook the rice according to the package directions.

4. While the rice is cooking, heat the coconut oil in a skillet. Add the scallions, ginger, and lemongrass and cook for 1 minute, then stir in the curry paste and cook for an additional minute.

5. Add the coconut milk and lentils and bring to a boil. Simmer for 15 minutes.

6. Drain the rice and add to the lentil mixture, along with the Tuscan kale. Simmer for 3–4 minutes.

7. Take the squash out of the oven and divide the lentil-and-rice mixture among the four halves.

8. Sprinkle with the sesame seeds and bake for an additional 10 minutes. Sprinkle with the cilantro leaves and serve.

DID YOU KNOW?
Tuscan kale is a dark-leafed Italian cabbage with many names, including cavelo nero and lacinato. If you can't find it, use its cousin kale instead.

PER SERVING: 626 CALS | 33.5G FAT | 21.2G SAT FAT | 72.6G CARBS | 9.7G SUGARS | 11.6G FIBER | 16.2G PROTEIN | 40MG SODIUM

BAKED CHICKEN WITH PEARS AND HAZELNUTS

*The combination of chicken and pears is an unusual one,
but it works well in this easy and healthy supper.*

SERVES: 4
PREP: 15 MINS   COOK: 30 MINS

4 skinless chicken breasts,
each weighing about 5 ounces
1½ tablespoons extra virgin canola oil
4 large shallots, cut into quarters
2 small pears, peeled, cored, and quartered
½ cup dry white wine
2 teaspoons garlic puree
2 teaspoons dried oregano
½ cup chicken broth
½ teaspoon salt
½ teaspoon pepper
⅓ cup blanched hazelnuts, finely chopped
2 tablespoons whole-wheat bread crumbs
2 tablespoons chopped fresh parsley
2 teaspoons fresh thyme leaves

1. Preheat the oven to 350°F. Cut each of the chicken breasts into two thick cutlets.

2. Put a large skillet over medium heat and add 1 tablespoon of the oil. Add the shallot quarters and sauté for 5 minutes, or until soft and light golden. Set aside until required.

3. Add the chicken and pears to the pan and cook over high heat for 2–3 minutes, turning once, until light golden (you may need to do this in two batches). Arrange the chicken in a large, shallow baking dish, tucking the shallots and pears around the edge.

4. Add the wine to the pan and bring to a boil. Stir in half the garlic and all the oregano, then stir in the broth, salt, and pepper. Pour the contents of the pan over the chicken mixture. Bake in the preheated oven for 15 minutes, basting the tops of the chicken pieces once or twice with the cooking juices.

5. Meanwhile, combine the hazelnuts, bread crumbs, parsley, and thyme with the remaining oil and garlic in a small bowl. Sprinkle the mixture over the top of the chicken and return to the oven for 10 minutes, or until the top has crisped a little and is lightly golden, and the chicken is tender and the juices run clear when the tip of a sharp knife is inserted into the thickest part of the meat. Serve immediately.

COOK'S TIP
This dish is good served with green beans and broccoli and also goes well with new potatoes in their skins.

PER SERVING: 350 CALS | 15.3G FAT | 1.7G SAT FAT | 16.9G CARBS | 6.5G SUGARS | 3.7G FIBER | 32.6G PROTEIN | 560MG SODIUM

BROILED CHICKEN
AND SLAW BOWL

Here's a perfect midweek meal for essential protein and energy, with crunchy vegetables drizzled in a spicy mayonnaise and topped with tender slices of chicken.

SERVES: 4

PREP: 18 MINS   COOK: 8–10 MINS

4 boneless, skinless chicken breasts,
about 5½ ounces each
1 teaspoon smoked paprika
salt and pepper (optional)
12 fresh arugula leaves, to garnish

COLESLAW

2 carrots, peeled and shredded
1 fennel bulb, trimmed and thinly sliced
1 beet, grated
1½ cups shredded red cabbage
15½ cups shredded green cabbage
4 radishes, thinly sliced
1 red onion, peeled and thinly sliced
¼ cup chopped fresh mixed herbs,
such as parsley, dill, mint, and cilantro
juice of 1 lemon
2 tablespoons extra virgin olive oil
1 cup plain yogurt
1 tablespoon whole-grain mustard

1. Preheat the broiler to medium heat.

2. To make the coleslaw, put all the coleslaw ingredients into a large bowl. Toss together well and set aside.

3. Place the chicken breasts between two sheets of wax paper and flatten with a rolling pin or mallet to a thickness of ½–¾ inch.

4. Season the chicken with paprika, and salt and pepper, if using. Broil for 4–5 minutes on each side, until the chicken is tender and the juices run clear when the tip of a sharp knife is inserted into the thickest part of the meat.

4. Divide the coleslaw among four bowls and top with slices of chicken breast and the arugula.

DID YOU KNOW?
Flattening the chicken breasts helps them to cook more quickly and evenly. Remove the skin, because this is where the fat is hidden.

PER SERVING: 362 CALS | 13.4G FAT | 3.1G SAT FAT | 21.9G CARBS | 12.7G SUGARS | 6.1G FIBER | 39.2G PROTEIN | 200MG SODIUM

LENTIL AND AMARANTH TABBOULEH

Amaranth is a high-quality source of plant protein, including the amino acids lysine and methionine. It's also bursting with iron and calcium, so it's an essential grain to have in your kitchen.

SERVES: 4

PREP: 25 MINS   COOK: 30 MINS

¾ cup amaranth
2 cups drained and rinsed, canned green lentils
or cooked green lentils
½ cucumber, diced
8 tomatoes, diced
1 small red onion, peeled and diced
⅓ cup chopped fresh parsley
⅓ cup chopped fresh mint
⅓ cup chopped fresh cilantro
1 cup toasted hazelnuts, chopped
5½ ounces halloumi cheese or Muenster cheese,
thickly sliced
salt and pepper (optional)
seeds from 1 pomegranate, to garnish
2 tablespoons coconut flakes, to garnish
2 tablespoons avocado oil, to serve

DRESSING
3 tablespoons olive oil
1 tablespoon balsamic vinegar
1 teaspoon whole-grain mustard
1 teaspoon honey

1. Cook the amaranth according to the package directions, until the grains are fluffy. Drain and let cool for a few minutes.

2. Meanwhile, make the dressing. Whisk together the olive oil, vinegar, mustard, and honey in a bowl.

3. Put the amaranth into a large bowl with the lentils, cucumber, tomatoes, onion, herbs, and hazelnuts. Pour over the dressing and toss together. Season with salt and pepper, if using, and let stand at room temperature.

4. In a dry skillet, cook the halloumi over medium heat, until golden on both sides.

5. Serve the halloumi with the tabbouleh, garnished with pomegranate seeds, coconut flakes, and a drizzle of avocado oil.

HELPFUL HAZELNUTS
Hazelnuts are a good source of protein and monounsaturated fats. They are also rich in the antioxidant vitamin E.

PER SERVING: 727 CALS | 47.1G FAT | 10.9G SAT FAT | 57.8G CARBS | 17.1G SUGARS | 12.8G FIBER | 23.5G PROTEIN | 480MG SODIUM

ONE-PAN SPICY CHICKEN

This dish is based on the gorgeous stews made in Morocco, using fruits (in this case, apricots, which are rich in iron) to add sweetness and a combination of spices for a fragrant sauce.

SERVES: 4
PREP: 15 MINS   COOK: 30–35 MINS

2 onions, peeled
1 tomato, halved
1¼-inch piece fresh ginger, peeled and chopped
3 garlic cloves, peeled
2 tablespoons olive oil
1½ pounds boneless, skinless chicken breasts,
cut into bite-size pieces
2 teaspoons ground cinnamon
1 teaspoon ground turmeric
2 teaspoons ground cumin
2 teaspoons ground coriander
1 large butternut squash, seeded and
cut into large pieces
¼ cup halved dried apricots
2½ cups chicken broth
1 cup red quinoa
¾ cup crumbled feta cheese
salt and pepper (optional)
⅓ cup chopped fresh mint leaves, to garnish

1. Chop 1 of the onions and put into a blender with the tomato, ginger, and garlic. Process to a puree.

2. Heat the olive oil in a large saucepan or casserole dish and cook the chicken over medium heat for 4–5 minutes, until browned all over. Remove from the pan and reserve.

3. Slice the remaining onion and cook in the same pan over medium heat for 3–4 minutes, then stir in the spices and cook for an additional minute.

4. Stir the onion and tomato puree into the pan and cook for 2 minutes.

5. Return the chicken to the pan with the squash, apricots, and broth. Simmer for 15–20 minutes, until the chicken is cooked through. Season with salt and pepper, if using.

6. Meanwhile, cook the quinoa according to the package directions.

7. Divide the chicken mixture and quinoa among four serving plates and sprinkle with feta and mint to serve.

WHY NOT TRY?
Other types of meat can be cooked this way—
for example, the recipe works well with pork loin.

PER SERVING: 656 CALS | 21.6G FAT | 7.2G SAT FAT | 71.3G CARBS | 15.6G SUGARS | 10.9G FIBER | 48.5G PROTEIN | 880MG SODIUM

QUINOA CHILI

Quinoa is a South American grain that contains all nine essential amino acids. It's easy to cook and is a great, wheat-free replacement for rice or couscous.

SERVES: 4
PREP: 12 MINS COOK: 36 MINS

$1/3$ cup red quinoa
1 tablespoon olive oil, for sautéing
1 onion, peeled and diced
2 green chiles, seeded and diced
$1\frac{1}{2}$ teaspoons smoked paprika
1 teaspoon chili powder
2 teaspoons cumin powder
$\frac{1}{2}$ teaspoon cayenne pepper
2 garlic cloves, crushed
$3\frac{1}{3}$ cups canned diced tomatoes
$1\frac{2}{3}$ cups drained and rinsed, canned kidney beans
$1\frac{2}{3}$ cups drained and rinsed, canned great Northern beans
$\frac{1}{2}$ cup water
$1/3$ cup chopped fresh cilantro leaves
2 tablespoons frozen corn kernels, thawed
2 tablespoons sour cream, to serve

1. Cook the quinoa according to the package directions.

2. Meanwhile, heat the oil in a separate large saucepan and sauté the onion over medium heat for 3–4 minutes to soften.

3. Add the chiles to the pan and cook for 1 minute. Stir in the spices and garlic, then cook for an additional 1 minute.

4. Drain the quinoa and add to the pan along with the tomatoes, beans, and water. Bring to a simmer and cook for 30 minutes, stirring occasionally, until thickened. Stir in half the cilantro leaves.

5. Divide the chili among four warm serving bowls and sprinkle the corn kernels and remaining cilantro over the top. Serve with the sour cream.

BOUNTIFUL BEANS
Kidney beans are an excellent source of protein, iron, and calcium for vegetarians and vegans. An average portion of kidney beans has at least one-quarter of our day's iron needs to help prevent anemia and increase energy levels, while their good zinc content helps boost the immune system.

PER SERVING: 277 CALS | 7.4G FAT | 1.3G SAT FAT | 38.6G CARBS | 10.5G SUGARS | 9.6G FIBER | 12.3G PROTEIN | 40MG SODIUM

TURKEY, SESAME, AND GINGER NOODLES

Turkey is one of the leanest meats you can buy and an invaluable source of protein. Unlike other meats, it also has a high amount of tryptophan, which can act as a mood stabilizer.

SERVES: 4
PREP: 10 MINS   COOK: 12 MINS

5½ ounces egg noodles
1 tablespoon olive oil, for frying
2 garlic cloves, crushed
1¼-inch piece fresh ginger, peeled and diced
14 ounces turkey breast, cut into strips
2 cups snow peas
1½ cups broccoli florets
1 red bell pepper, seeded and sliced
2 scallions, trimmed and sliced
1½ cups bean sprouts
1 tablespoon sesame oil
1 tablespoon soy sauce
1 tablespoon sweet chili sauce
juice of ½ lime
⅓ cup smooth peanut butter
⅔ cup roasted peanuts, chopped
⅓ cup fresh cilantro leaves, to garnish

1. Cook the egg noodles according to the package directions.

2. Heat the olive oil in a wok or large skillet and add the garlic, ginger, and turkey. Stir-fry over medium heat for 3–4 minutes, until the turkey is cooked through. Remove from the pan and reserve.

3. Add the snow peas, broccoli, and red bell pepper to the wok and stir-fry over medium heat for 4–5 minutes. Add the scallions and bean sprouts, and continue to cook for 1 minute.

4. Whisk together the sesame oil, soy sauce, chili sauce, lime juice, and peanut butter in a small bowl and add to the wok along with the turkey and noodles. Toss together well.

5. Divide the turkey and noodles among four warm serving bowls and top with the peanuts and cilantro to serve.

COOK'S TIP
This dish is delicious eaten hot or cold. Take any leftovers to work the next day for an easy lunch.

PER SERVING: 675 CALS | 35.6G FAT | 6.2G SAT FAT | 50.2G CARBS | 11.5G SUGARS | 7.8G FIBER | 44.2G PROTEIN | 520MG SODIUM

BULGUR WHEAT BALLS WITH CHICKPEA HUMMUS

*These vegetarian "wheat balls" are just as delicious as meatballs.
Made from bulgur wheat and served with a velvety chickpea
and walnut hummus, this is a nutritious family meal.*

SERVES: 4
PREP: 20 MINS, PLUS CHILLING   COOK: 25–30 MINS

1⅓ cups bulgur wheat
1 small red onion, peeled and diced
2 teaspoons ground cumin
2 teaspoons ground turmeric
½ teaspoon smoked paprika
⅓ cup chopped fresh cilantro
2 eggs, beaten
2 tablespoons olive oil, for frying
2 tablespoons sesame seeds, toasted, to garnish
2 cups fresh watercress, to serve

CHICKPEA HUMMUS

1⅔ cups drained and rinsed, canned chickpeas
½ cup toasted walnuts
1 garlic clove, crushed
juice of 1 lemon
½ cup extra virgin olive oil
salt and pepper (optional)

1. Bring a large saucepan of water to a boil. Add the bulgur wheat and cook for 20 minutes, or according to package directions, until soft. Drain and refresh under cold running water.

2. In a bowl, mix together the bulgur wheat, onion, spices, cilantro, and eggs.

3. Shape the mixture into 12 walnut-size balls using your hands. Place them on a plate and chill in the refrigerator for 30 minutes.

4. Meanwhile, make the hummus. Put the chickpeas and walnuts into a food processor and process until they resemble bread crumbs.

5. Add the garlic and lemon juice to the processor and process again.

6. With the machine running, gradually add the extra virgin olive oil until you have a smooth consistency. Season with salt and pepper, if using. Transfer the hummus to a bowl and set aside.

7. Heat the olive oil in a skillet and cook the balls over medium heat for 3–4 minutes, occasionally turning them to brown all over.

8. Serve the bulgur wheat balls on a bed of watercress, topped with a dollop of hummus and sprinkled with toasted sesame seeds.

WHY NOT TRY?
For another great hummus recipe, swap the walnuts for a peeled and chopped avocado—it tastes heavenly and is full of healthy fats.

PER SERVING: 700 CALS | 46.3G FAT | 6G SAT FAT | 55.1G CARBS | 4.4G SUGARS | 14.7G FIBER | 18.3G PROTEIN | 80MG SODIUM

PAN-FRIED TUNA WITH SEAWEED PESTO

You may associate seaweed with Japanese cuisine, but it's actually a versatile ingredient. It's highly nutritious and one of the few ingredients that's rich in iodine, which is important for thyroid health.

SERVES: 4
PREP: 20 MINS   COOK: 25 MINS

4 tuna steaks, about 5½ ounces each
4 teaspoons black pepper
1 tablespoon olive oil
2 cups fresh watercress

SWEET POTATO WEDGES

2 sweet potatoes, cut into wedges
3 tablespoons olive oil
¼ teaspoon smoked paprika
salt and pepper (optional)

SEAWEED PESTO

1½ cups dried wakame, soaked in water
for 20 minutes, until rehydrated, drained
½ garlic clove, chopped
2½ tablepsoons toasted pine nuts
3 tablespoons grated pecorino cheese
juice of ½ lemon
⅓ cup extra virgin olive oil

1. Preheat the oven to 400°F.

2. To make the sweet potato wedges, toss the sweet potato wedges in a bowl with the olive oil and paprika. Season with salt and pepper, if using, then spread across a baking sheet or roasting pan.

3. Roast the sweet potato in the preheated oven for 15–20 minutes, until tender.

4. Meanwhile, make the seaweed pesto. Put the rehydrated wakame into a food processor with the garlic and pine nuts, and process to break down.

5. Add the cheese and lemon juice to the processor and pulse again.

6. With the machine running, slowly add the extra virgin olive oil until you have a pesto consistency. Transfer to a bowl and set aside.

7. Season each tuna steak with 1 teaspoon of black pepper. Make sure both sides are seasoned.

8. Heat the olive oil in a skillet and cook the tuna over high heat for 3–4 minutes on each side, depending on how pink you prefer it.

9. Serve the pan-fried tuna with a dollop of seaweed pesto, the sweet potato wedges, and watercress.

SWEET POTATO POWER
Sweet potatoes are richer in nutrients than potatoes and lower on the glycemic index.

PER SERVING: 602 CALS | 41.4G FAT | 6G SAT FAT | 17.1G CARBS | 3.1G SUGARS | 2.8G FIBER | 40.2G PROTEIN | 240MG SODIUM

MIXED BEAN, NUT, AND KALE STEW

Kale is a wonderfully nourishing vegetable, rich in vitamin B6, fiber, potassium, magnesium, and more. Served with protein-packed beans, this is a dinner the entire family will enjoy.

SERVES: 4

PREP: 10 MINS COOK: 30 MINS

1 tablespoon olive oil, for sautéing

1 large onion, peeled and chopped

2 garlic cloves, peeled and sliced

1 teaspoon smoked paprika

1⅓ cups fava beans

1⅔ cups drained and rinsed, canned lima beans

1 cup trimmed and halved green beans

1⅔ cups canned diced tomatoes

1 cup vegetable broth

2 cups shredded kale

2 tablespoons chopped walnuts

1 tablespoon chopped Brazil nuts

1 tablespoon chopped hazelnuts

1 cup crumbled feta cheese

salt and pepper (optional)

1 tablespoon chopped fresh mint, to garnish

1 tablespoon extra virgin olive oil, to serve

1. Heat the olive oil in a large saucepan and sauté the onion over medium heat for 2–3 minutes. Stir in the garlic and paprika, and cook for an additional minute.

2. Stir the beans, tomatoes, and broth into the pan and bring to a simmer. Cook for 15 minutes, then stir in the kale and cook for an additional 10 minutes. Season with salt and pepper, if using.

3. Toast the nuts in a dry saucepan over medium heat for 2–3 minutes.

4. Ladle the stew into four bowls and serve topped with the toasted nuts, feta, chopped mint, and a drizzle of olive oil.

COOK'S TIP

If you can get fava beans in season, they are preferable for this recipe. If not, substitute with frozen fava beans.

PER SERVING: 408 CALS | 23.1G FAT | 8.4G SAT FAT | 30.5G CARBS | 9.7G SUGARS | 10.1G FIBER | 19.5G PROTEIN | 600MG SODIUM

MISO STEAK AND BELL PEPPER STIR-FRY

*Steak is high in protein but also contains saturated fat,
so it's important to pick lean cuts and not eat red meat
too often. Instead, try to fill up on different fish and vegetables.*

SERVES: 4
PREP: 15 MINS, PLUS CHILLING   COOK: 15 MINS

12 ounces lean tenderloin steaks
1 tablespoon melted coconut oil, for frying
4 scallions, cut into 1½-inch lengths
¾-inch piece fresh ginger, peeled and grated
1 carrot, peeled and cut into matchsticks
1 red bell pepper, seeded and sliced
1 yellow bell pepper, seeded and sliced
7 baby corn, halved
1 zucchini, cut into matchsticks
1 cup shredded snow peas
1 tablespoon soy sauce
2 tablespoons sesame seeds, to garnish

MARINADE
2 tablespoons brown miso paste
1 tablespoon sake
1 tablespoon sugar
2 garlic cloves, crushed

1. To make the marinade, mix the marinade ingredients together in a nonmetallic bowl. Add the steaks and rub all over with the mixture. Cover and chill in the refrigerator for at least 1 hour (the longer the better).

2. Heat a ridged grill pan and cook the steaks over medium heat for 2–3 minutes on each side, depending on how pink you prefer your steak. Remove from the pan and let rest.

3. Meanwhile, heat the coconut oil in a wok or large skillet and cook the scallions and ginger over medium heat for 2 minutes.

4. Add the carrot, bell peppers, and corn to the wok and stir-fry for 2 minutes, then add the zucchini and snow peas. Stir-fry for an additional 3 minutes.

5. Slice the steaks and add to the wok with the soy sauce. Stir-fry for 1 minute, until all the vegetables are cooked but not soft.

6. Divide the steak slices and vegetables among four plates and sprinkle with sesame seeds. Serve immediately.

PROTECTIVE PEPPERS
The bright colors of bell peppers contain high levels of carotenes for heart health and cancer protection, and are also a rich source of vitamin C.

PER SERVING: 260 CALS | 9.1G FAT | 4.2G SAT FAT | 18.5G CARBS | 11.2G SUGARS | 4.5G FIBER | 26.2G PROTEIN | 600MG SODIUM

DESSERTS AND BAKING

BLACK RICE PUDDING

Black rice turns a classic pudding into a stylish, contemporary dish. A great source of iron, vitamin E, and antioxidants, it's also higher in fiber and protein than white or brown rice.

SERVES: 4
PREP: 8 MINS   COOK: 25 MINS

¾ cup black rice
½ cup soy light cream
1 thick slice fresh pineapple, halved
6 knobs preserved ginger, diced
¼ cup preserve ginger syrup
⅓ cup shredded fresh mint leaves
¼ cup coconut yogurt

1. Cook the rice according to the package directions.

2. Drain the rice and put three-quarters of it into a food processor with the soy cream and half the pineapple. Process until you have the consistency of rice pudding.

3. Spoon the rice mixture into four glasses.

4. Dice the remaining pineapple and put into a bowl with the diced ginger, syrup, and mint. Mix well.

5. Spoon the coconut yogurt over the rice mixture, then pour over the ginger-and-pineapple mixture to serve.

PERFECT PINEAPPLE
Pineapples are a good source of vitamin C and other vitamins and minerals, including magnesium.

PER SERVING: 277 CALS | 6.9G FAT | 3.2G SAT FAT | 48.3G CARBS | 15.3G SUGARS | 3G FIBER | 5.7G PROTEIN | TRACE SODIUM

MATCHA CASHEW CREAM TARTS

Matcha is a stone-ground green tea traditionally used in Japanese tea ceremonies. Aside from its various vitamins and minerals, it's valued for polyphenol compounds called catechins—antioxidants that help fight disease.

MAKES: 8 TARTS
PREP: 20 MINS, PLUS CHILLING   COOK: NONE

⅓ cup coconut oil, melted,
plus 1 tablespoon for oiling
6 dates, pitted
½ cup coconut flour
1 cup dry unsweetened coconut
2½ tablespoons ground almonds (almond meal)
1 teaspoon matcha powder

CASHEW CREAM
¾ cup cashew nuts, soaked in boiling water for
15 minutes, drained and rinsed
¼ cup water
1 tablespoon maple syrup
2 tablespoons plain yogurt
1 banana, peeled and sliced
2 passion fruits, pulp only, to decorate

1. Oil an 8-cup muffin pan with coconut oil and line with paper liners. Set aside.

2. Pour the melted coconut oil into a food processor with the dates, coconut flour, dry coconut, ground almonds, and matcha powder. Process until the batter is well combined.

3. Divide the batter among the liners in the prepared pan and press down, making little tarts. Chill in the refrigerator for at least 1 hour.

4. Meanwhile, make your cashew cream. Put the soaked nuts into a food processor with the water and maple syrup. Blend until just combined.

5. Add the yogurt and half the banana slices to the processor and continue to blend until smooth.

6. Remove the chilled tarts from the pan and spoon a dollop of the cashew cream onto each one. Decorate each tart with a few slices of banana and a little passion fruit pulp.

GOOD-FOR-YOU CASHEWS
High in monounsaturated fats, cashew nuts help protect the heart, and they contain a range of minerals for strong bones, improved immunity, and increased energy levels.

PER TART: 293 CALS | 23.3G FAT | 15.2G SAT FAT | 18.2G CARBS | 10.2G SUGARS | 5.5G FIBER | 5G PROTEIN | TRACE SODIUM

FROZEN YOGURT BARK

*If you're struggling to think of healthy treats for your children,
this frozen yogurt dessert makes a great after-school snack and will
replace potato chips and candy with an assortment of fruits and nuts.*

SERVES: 4

PREP: 10 MINS, PLUS FREEZING   COOK: NONE

2 cups Greek-style yogurt
2 tablespoons maple syrup
zest of 1 orange
1/3 cup blueberries
1/3 cup dried cherries
3/4 cup coarsely chopped pistachio nuts
3/4 cup raspberries

1. Line a 6¼ x 10½-inch shallow pan with parchment paper, leaving extra paper hanging over the rim (this will help you lift the bark out once frozen). Set aside.

2. Put the yogurt, maple syrup, orange zest, blueberries, and cherries into a large bowl and mix together.

3. Pour the yogurt mixture into the prepared pan and make sure the fruit is evenly dispersed.

4. Sprinkle the chopped pistachio nuts and raspberries on top of the yogurt. Freeze for at least 2 hours, or until completely frozen.

5. Remove the bark from the pan with the overhanging pieces of paper and cut into shapes of your choice.

INCREASED POWER

To increase the protein content, you could stir
some nut butter through the yogurt.

PER SERVING: 349 CALS | 17.9G FAT | 6G SAT FAT | 33.4G CARBS | 23.5G SUGARS | 5G FIBER | 16.9G PROTEIN | 40MG SODIUM

NO-BAKE BERRY CHEESECAKE

There's no baking required for this beautiful cheesecake—just put it into the refrigerator. You can try adding different toppings, such as mango and passion fruit; oranges and preserved ginger; or pomegranate and pistachio nuts.

SERVES: 8
PREP: 20 MINS, PLUS CHILLING   COOK: NONE

1 tablespoon melted coconut oil, for oiling
½ cup walnuts
⅔ cup ground almonds (almond meal)
8 Medjool dates, pitted
1 tablespoon melted coconut oil

FILLING
2½ cups cream cheese
grated zest of 2 lemons
¾ cup confectioners' sugar
½ cup heavy cream
1 cup Greek-style yogurt

TOPPING
¾ cup blueberries
⅔ cup raspberries
⅔ cup hulled and halved strawberries
1 tablespoon cacao nibs, to decorate (optional)
⅓ cup fresh mint leaves, to decorate

1. Lightly oil a 9-inch springform cake pan with coconut oil and set aside.

2. Put the walnuts, ground almonds, and dates into a food processor and process until they are broken down to a fine crumb. While the machine is running, pour in the second tablespoon of coconut oil.

3. Press the crumb mixture into the bottom of the prepared pan.

4. To make the filling, put the cream cheese, lemon zest, and confectioners' sugar into a bowl and, using a handheld mixer, beat until smooth. Add the cream and yogurt, and continue to beat until the mixture is combined and stiff.

5. Spoon the cream-cheese filling onto the crust and chill in the refrigerator for at least 3 hours.

6. Remove the cheesecake from the pan and place on a serving plate. Sprinkle with the blueberries and raspberries.

7. Puree the strawberries in a small blender and drizzle over the top of the cheesecake. Decorate with mint leaves and cacao nibs, if using, to serve.

MAKE IT CHOCOLATEY
To make a no-bake chocolate cheesecake, add 1 tablespoon of cocoa powder to the crust and swirl 5½ ounces melted semisweet chocolate over the top before sprinkling with mint and cacao nibs.

PER SERVING: 593 CALS | 44.6G FAT | 23.4G SAT FAT | 43.5G CARBS | 35.9G SUGARS | 4.5G FIBER | 10.5G PROTEIN | 240MG SODIUM

CHOCOLATE YOGURT POPS

Instead of buying sugar-laden ice pops, make these naturally sweet chocolate yogurt pops. They'll be a huge success on hot summer days.

MAKES: 10 POPS
PREP: 20 MINS, PLUS FREEZING   COOK: NONE

1⅓ cups Greek-style yogurt
2 bananas, peeled and mashed
4 teaspoons honey
10½ ounces semisweet chocolate, chopped
½ cup coconut oil
3½ ounces milk chocolate, chopped
3½ ounces white chocolate, chopped
1 tablespoon chopped pistachio nuts

YOU WILL ALSO NEED:
10 (3-ounce) ice pop molds
10 ice pop sticks

1. Put the yogurt into a bowl with the mashed banana and honey. Mix well.

2. Pour the yogurt mixture into ten 3-ounce ice pop molds. Insert the ice pop sticks and freeze for at least 2 hours.

3. Gently melt the semisweet chocolate and coconut oil in a heatproof bowl placed over a saucepan of simmering water. Don't let the bowl touch the water.

4. Melt the milk chocolate in the same way as the semisweet chocolate.

5. Remove the ice pops from the molds and dip them into the melted semisweet chocolate-and-coconut oil mixture, then return to the freezer for a couple of minutes to set.

6. To decorate the ice pops, swirl the melted milk chocolate around each one with a fork, then sprinkle with white chocolate and pistachio nuts. Return to the freezer to set.

DID YOU KNOW?
Bananas are antacids, lowering the distress associated with heartburn, stomachaches, and acid reflux.

PER POP: 438 CALS | 29.7G FAT | 19.9G SAT FAT | 36.7G CARBS | 28.5G SUGARS | 3.5G FIBER | 6.5G PROTEIN | 40MG SODIUM

CHOCOLATE AND CHIA PUDDINGS

Coconut milk and plain yogurt add an appealing creaminess to these chilled chocolate puddings, plus agave syrup sweetens them naturally and on-trend chia seeds add that extra nutrient boost.

SERVES: 3
PREP: 20 MINS, PLUS CHILLING   COOK: NONE

2 tablespoons cocoa powder
2 tablespoons agave syrup
⅓ cup coconut milk
½ cup Greek-style plain yogurt
2 tablespoons chia seeds
1 teaspoon vanilla extract
1 kiwi, sliced, to decorate
1¾ ounces semisweet chocolate, coarsely chopped, to decorate

1: Put the cocoa powder and agave syrup into a large bowl and mix well to remove any lumps. Stir in the coconut milk, Greek yogurt, chia seeds, and vanilla extract and mix thoroughly.

2: Cover and refrigerate for 4–6 hours. Remove the mixture from the refrigerator; it should be thick at this stage. Using an electric handheld mixer, blend the mixture until smooth, then carefully divide among three small dessert glasses.

3: Chill the puddings for an additional hour. Decorate with the kiwi slices and semisweet chocolate and serve.

SKIN-SOOTHING KIWI
Kiwis are full of omega-3, which is important in preventing an array of skin diseases and protecting the health of cell membranes. As a strong provider of vitamin C and vitamin E, kiwis help to maintain the skin's moisture and aid the healing of cuts and scars.

PER SERVING: 307 CALS | 18.8G FAT | 11.8G SAT FAT | 29.7G CARBS | 18.7G SUGARS | 7G FIBER | 7.9G PROTEIN | TRACE SODIUM

HEALTHY COOKIE DOUGH DIP

This cookie dough isn't what it seems: mixing lima beans with semisweet chocolate and almond makes a delicious dip but without all the refined sugar and calories.

SERVES: 4
PREP: 8–10 MINS   COOK: NONE

1²/₃ cups drained and rinsed, canned lima beans
½ teaspoon baking soda
3 drops vanilla extract
2 tablespoons almond butter
1 tablespoon almond milk
1 tablespoon ground flaxseed
½ teaspoon honey, plus extra to taste (optional)
1³/₄ ounces semisweet chocolate, chopped
sliced fresh fruits, such as banana, strawberries, pear, mango, and melon, to serve (optional)

1. Put all the ingredients, except the chocolate, into a food processor and process until nearly smooth. Add a little more honey if you'd prefer the dip to be sweeter.

2. Stir the chopped chocolate into the dip and serve with the fruit of your choice, if using.

COOK'S TIP
You can use other white beans, or chickpeas, if you don't have any lima beans.

PER SERVING: 198 CALS | 10.4G FAT | 3.4G SAT FAT | 18.5G CARBS | 6.3G SUGARS | 5.4G FIBER | 7.1G PROTEIN | 160MG SODIUM

CHOCOLATE AND ALMOND BISCOTTI

Biscotti are Italian cookies baked twice for a crunchy coating that are traditionally served with coffee. These are made with almonds for protein, calcium, and potassium, and they are decorated with chocolate drizzle.

MAKES: 22 BISCOTTI
PREP: 15 MINS   COOK: 50–60 MINS

1 teaspoon baking powder
1¼ cups all-purpose flour
¾ cup buckwheat flour
¾ cup superfine or granulated sugar
¼ cup cacao powder
¼ teaspoon ground cinnamon
4 eggs, beaten
1¼ cups blanched almonds,
toasted and coarsely chopped
3½ ounces semisweet chocolate, to decorate
3½ ounces white chocolate, to decorate

1. Preheat the oven to 300°F. Line a baking sheet with parchment paper and set aside.

2. Put the baking powder, flours, sugar, cacao powder, and cinnamon into a large bowl and stir together.

3. Add the eggs to the bowl and stir into the dry ingredients, adding the almonds once the dough starts coming together.

4. Turn the dough out onto a floured work surface and roll it into a long log shape, about 14 inches long and 2½–2¾ inches wide. Place on the prepared baking sheet and bake in the preheated oven for 30–40 minutes.

5. Remove the sheet from the oven and cool on a rack for 10 minutes.

6. Cut the dough into ½-inch-thick slices and bake for an additional 8–10 minutes on each side, until firm. Cool on a rack.

7. Gently melt the semisweet chocolate and white chocolate in separate heatproof bowls over saucepans of simmering water. Don't let the bowls touch the water. Once melted, drizzle lines of chocolate over the biscotti to decorate. Let set before serving.

WHY NOT TRY?
Add dried fruits, such as cranberries or chopped apricots, for extra sweetness.

PER BISCOTTI: 178 CALS | 8.6G FAT | 2.6G SAT FAT | 22.3G CARBS | 11.7G SUGARS | 2.2G FIBER | 4.7G PROTEIN | 40MG SODIUM

RASPBERRY, CHIA SEED, AND PECAN CUPS

Chia seeds may be tiny, but they're packed with protein, fiber, and omega-3 fats. In addition to the health boost, they give juices and pureed fruits gorgeous texture.

SERVES: 4
PREP: 10 MINS   COOK: NONE

3¼ cups raspberries
2 tablespoons chia seeds
1 mango, pitted, peeled, and chopped
1¾ cups Greek-style yogurt
3 kiwis, peeled and sliced
2 tablespoons pecans, toasted and coarsely chopped, to decorate

1. Put the raspberries into a food processor and process until smooth, then transfer to a bowl. Stir in the chia seeds and let stand—the chia seeds will gradually thicken the mixture to a preserve-like consistency.

2. Put the mango into a clean processor and process until smooth. Lightly stir through the yogurt, leaving trails of the mango showing.

3. Layer the yogurt, raspberry-chia mixture, and kiwi slices in four glasses, finishing with yogurt on top.

4. Sprinkle the dessert with chopped pecans to serve.

AMAZING MANGO
A mango is 14 percent natural sugar, and this can be quickly converted into energy by the body. It is also rich in beta-carotene and vitamin C.

PER SERVING: 281 CALS | 10.8G FAT | 4.1G SAT FAT | 37.7G CARBS | 23.2G SUGARS | 11.8G FIBER | 12.8G PROTEIN | 40MG SODIUM

TOFU LEMON CHEESECAKE

Fiber-filled dates and naturally sweet agave syrup add flavor and appeal to the crunchy gingersnap crust, then zesty lemons add the finest refreshing flavor to the topping of this top-notch chilled cheesecake.

SERVES: 10
PREP: 30–35 MINS, PLUS CHILLING   COOK: 5 MINS

CRUST
1 cup pecans
7 soft dried dates
12 gingersnaps
2 tablespoons agave syrup
1 tablespoon lemon zest, to decorate

FILLING
12 ounces firm silken tofu, excess water drained
1¼ cups cream cheese
⅓ cup Greek-style plain yogurt
juice and grated zest of 3 lemons
½ cup firmly packed light brown sugar
½ teaspoon vanilla extract
2 tablespoons powdered gelatin
⅓ cup cold water

1. Line an 8-inch round springform baking pan with parchment paper.

2. To make the crust, put the pecans, dates, cookies, and agave syrup into a food processor and pulse until the mixture comes together. The dough should be slightly sticky when rolled in your hands. Empty the dough into the bottom of your prepared pan and press down to create an even crust.

3. To make the filling, put the tofu into a food processor with the cream cheese, yogurt, lemon juice, lemon zest, brown sugar, and vanilla extract. Blend until silky smooth.

4. Put the powdered gelatin into a small bowl and pour the cold water over it. Set the bowl over a saucepan filled with gently simmering water. Stir the gelatin until it has dissolved into the liquid and, working quickly, pour the liquid gelatin into the filling mixture. Blend the filling again until the gelatin is completely incorporated.

5. Spoon the filling on top of the crust and place in the refrigerator to chill for 6 hours or overnight. Serve in slices, decorated with lemon zest.

PER SERVING: 368 CALS | 22.2G FAT | 7.7G SAT FAT | 37.6G CARBS | 29.7G SUGARS | 2.9G FIBER | 8.4G PROTEIN | 160MG SODIUM

PEANUT BUTTER AND BANANA MUFFINS

These lovely muffins are healthier than most store-bought ones and can be eaten as a guilt-free dessert after dinner or taken to work for an easy breakfast.

MAKES: 12 MUFFINS
PREP: 12 MINS   COOK: 15–20 MINS

1$\frac{2}{3}$ cups all–purpose flour
$\frac{1}{3}$ cup plus 1 tablespoon buckwheat flour
1$\frac{1}{2}$ teaspoons baking powder
$\frac{1}{3}$ cup superfine or granulated sugar
$\frac{1}{3}$ cup rolled oats
2 bananas, peeled and mashed
$\frac{1}{3}$ cup chunky peanut butter
2 eggs, beaten
2 tablespoons melted coconut oil
$\frac{1}{2}$ cup milk

1. Preheat the oven to 400° F. Line a 12–cup muffin pan with paper liners and set aside.

2. Sift the flours, baking powder, and sugar into a large bowl, then mix in the oats.

3. In a separate bowl, mix the mashed banana and peanut butter with the eggs, melted coconut oil, and milk.

4. Stir the banana mixture into the flour mixture, but do not overmix. The tastiest muffins are made from the lumpiest batter.

5. Spoon the batter into the prepared muffin liners and bake in the preheated oven for 15–18 minutes, until risen and golden.

COOK'S TIP
Almond butter or other nut butters
can also be used in this recipe.

PER MUFFIN: 214 CALS | 8.3G FAT | 3.2G SAT FAT | 30.1G CARBS | 10.1G SUGARS | 2.3G FIBER | 6.1G PROTEIN | 240MG SODIUM

CHOCOLATE ORANGE MUG CAKE

*There are times when all you want is some instant gratification,
so here's a cake made in less than 10 minutes, with a tasty
chocolate and orange cake and almond butter for protein!*

SERVES: 1
PREP: 3 MINS   COOK: 2 MINS

1½ tablespoons almond butter
1 heaping tablespoon chickpea (besan) flour
1 heaping tablespoon cocoa powder
½ teaspoon baking powder
2 teaspoons superfine or granulated sugar
1 extra-large egg
grated zest of 1 orange
1 tablespoon Greek-style yogurt, to serve

1. Put all the ingredients, except half the orange zest and the yogurt, into a large microwave-proof mug and mix together well with a teaspoon.

2. Bake in the microwave for 2 minutes, until risen and cooked through.

3. Serve the mug cake with a dollop of yogurt and a sprinkling of orange zest.

MIX IT UP
Use the basic recipe and add your own choice of flavors—chopped banana or mango work well.

PER SERVING: 361 CALS | 20.2G FAT | 4.5G SAT FAT | 31.5G CARBS | 12.7G SUGARS | 7.9G FIBER | 19.6G PROTEIN | 360MG SODIUM

INDEX